Dear Parent:
Your child's love of reading starts here!

Every child learns to read in a different way and at his or her own speed. Some go back and forth between reading levels and read favorite books again and again. Others read through each level in order. You can help your young reader improve and become more confident by encouraging his or her own interests and abilities. From books your child reads with you to the first books he or she reads alone, there are I Can Read Books for every stage of reading:

SHARED READING
Basic language, word repetition, and whimsical illustrations, ideal for sharing with your emergent reader

BEGINNING READING
Short sentences, familiar words, and simple concepts for children eager to read on their own

READING WITH HELP
Engaging stories, longer sentences, and language play for developing readers

READING ALONE
Complex plots, challenging vocabulary, and high-interest topics for the independent reader

ADVANCED READING
Short paragraphs, chapters, and exciting themes for the perfect bridge to chapter books

I Can Read Books have introduced children to the joy of reading since 1957. Featuring award-winning authors and illustrators and a fabulous cast of beloved characters, I Can Read Books set the standard for beginning readers.

A lifetime of discovery begins with the magical words "I Can Read!"

Visit www.icanread.com for information
on enriching your child's reading experience.

Ree Drummond and Diane deGroat gratefully acknowledge the editorial and artistic contributions of Amanda Glickman and Rick Whipple.

I Can Read Book® is a trademark of HarperCollins Publishers.

Charlie the Ranch Dog: Where's the Bacon? Text copyright © 2013 by Ree Drummond. Cover art copyright © 2013 by Diane deGroat. Interior art copyright © 2013 by HarperCollins Publishers. All rights reserved. Manufactured in China. No part of this book may be used or reproduced in any manner whatsoever without written permission except in the case of brief quotations embodied in critical articles and reviews. For information address HarperCollins Children's Books, a division of HarperCollins Publishers, 10 East 53rd Street, New York, NY 10022.
www.icanread.com

Library of Congress catalog card number: 2012949619
ISBN 978-0-06-221909-1 (trade bdg.) —ISBN 978-0-06-221908-4 (pbk.)

13 14 15 16 17   SCP   10 9 8 7 6 5 4 3 2 1   ❖   First Edition

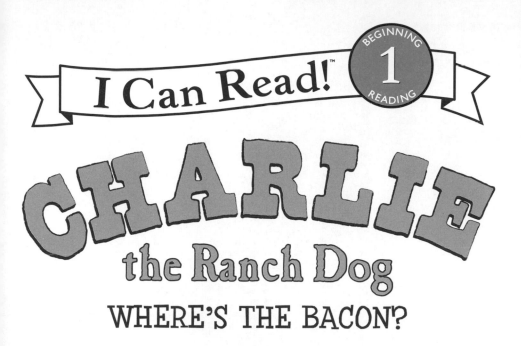

I Can Read!

BEGINNING 1 READING

CHARLIE
the Ranch Dog
WHERE'S THE BACON?

based on the CHARLIE THE RANCH DOG books
by REE DRUMMOND, The Pioneer Woman
and DIANE deGROAT

HARPER
An Imprint of HarperCollinsPublishers

Oh, hello.

I'm Charlie.

This is my ranch.

I'm the boss around here.

This is Rowdy.

He doesn't live here.

He's just visiting

while his family is away

for a couple of days.

I don't normally have time
for visitors.
After all, I have work to do!
But I'll be a good boss man
and show Rowdy around the ranch.

Everything will be okay as long as

Rowdy doesn't get too rowdy.

I run a tight ship

around this place.

I give a sniff, sniff,

just to say hello.

Hmm. That's funny.

Rowdy smells like bacon.

He must like bacon, too.

That reminds me. It's breakfast time!

(Breakfast is my life.)

I run into the kitchen.

Huh? Excuse me?

My bacon is gone!

My water bowl is empty, too.

Sniff.

Sniff, sniff.

Sniff, sniff, sniff.

I walk around and around.

My nose follows the trail of bacon.

I run right into Rowdy!

He's standing in my personal space.

I wonder if he's ever even heard

of personal space!

My belly rumbles.

What a bad morning for a ranch dog.

No bacon. No water.

No personal space.

Huh?

Where did Rowdy go?

I don't see him anywhere.

I hope he's not being rowdy!

I find Rowdy.

He's playing in the garden.

He lies down next to Mama.

She rubs his belly.

MAMA?!?

Okay, this is going too far.

I give Rowdy "the look."

He runs past me into the house.

I sniff, sniff.

"Hey, you bacon eater!" I shout.

"Get back here!"

Mama loves my short legs,
but they are not the best
for running fast.
Soon Rowdy is out of my sight again.

Visitors are difficult!

All this running around is tiring.

After all this trouble,

I think I'll just go inside,

lie down, and take a little snooze.

Who is that in my bed?

ROWDY!

That's it. A ranch dog can only
take so much.

21

Rowdy jumps off the bed.

He runs out the door

and skips down the steps.

His tail is between his legs.

He dives into the doghouse.

Oh, Rowdy.

Now I feel bad.

I didn't mean to scare the big guy.

But goodness me,

Rowdy is hard to manage!

Eating my bacon,

drinking my water,

getting belly rubs from my mama,

and the final straw: sleeping in my bed!

Ahh. Nice and cozy.

Finally, I can get a little rest.

Hmm.

That's funny.

I don't feel very sleepy.

I think about Rowdy.

I wonder if he's lonely

outside in the doghouse.

Hey.

Sniff, sniff, sniff.

Something smells good!

What's for dinner?

Mama gives me a soup bone,

and I know just what to do with it.

When I walk up to the doghouse,

I hear Rowdy crying.

Poor fella.

"I'm sorry, Rowdy," I say.

"You must miss your mama."

Rowdy gives me a sniff, sniff.

And a lick, lick.

"Maybe there's room on this ranch
for the both of us," I say.
Then I share my dinner
with my new friend.

After dinner, I feel sleepy.

"Time for a nap, Rowdy?" I ask.

I even let him share my sofa.

Zzzzzzzzzzzzz.